Spirituality
for Ministry

Spirituality *for* Ministry

Seven Perspectives

James J. Bacik
Doris Donnelly
Michael Downey
Edward P. Hahnenberg
Patricia H. Livingston
Ronald Rolheiser
Susan K. Wood

Edited by Karen Sue Smith

Liguori
LIGUORI, MISSOURI

Imprimi Potest:
Thomas D. Picton, C.Ss.R.
Provincial, Denver Province
The Redemptorists

Published by Liguori Publications
Liguori, Missouri
www.liguori.org

The essays in this volume originally appeared in *Church* magazine, published by the National Pastoral Life Center, New York City, New York, a journal that promotes excellence among pastors and parish leaders.

Library of Congress Cataloging-in-Publication Data

Spirituality for ministry : seven perspectives / James J. Bacik ... [et al.] ; edited by Karen Sue Smith.
      p. cm.
    ISBN-13: 978-0-7648-1512-6 ; ISBN-10: 0-7648-1512-1
    1. Spirituality—Catholic Church. 2. Pastoral theology. 3. Lay ministry—Catholic Church. I. Bacik, James J., 1936– II. Smith, Karen Sue.
    BX2350.65.S68 2006
    248.8'9—dc22   2006025573

Liguori Publications, a nonprofit corporation, is an apostolate of the Redemptorists. To learn more about the Redemptorists, visit *Redemptorists.com*.

Printed in the United States of America
10 09 08 07 06   5 4 3 2 1
First edition

Acknowledgments

The essays in this volume originally appeared in *Church* magazine, published by the National Pastoral Life Center, New York City, a journal that promotes excellence among pastors and parish leaders. Inspired by subscribers who sought permission to photocopy the series or asked for a specific issue they had missed, Liguori Publications graciously agreed to publish the essays in one volume. Liguori Publications extends special thanks to *Church* magazine, particularly to the editor of this book, Karen Sue Smith.

Contents

Introduction

P erhaps every age is a thrilling time in which to practice one's faith, but our age seems especially so to me.
We Catholics are in the midst of a transition concern-
ing what ministry is and who performs it. Since ministry
lies at the heart of the Gospel (it is the way we followers of Jesus carry out his mission in the world), it is the
Church's, and our own, *raison d'être*. It encompasses the
way we live and work, pray and worship, play and dream.
It is important, then, to reflect on the two basic questions:
What is ministry? and Who performs it? If the reflection proceeds well, more clarity will gradually emerge.

On the human level, the Catholic Church can be described as a complex, hierarchical institution, which, at the
ripe old age of roughly two millennia, has outlived most
other institutions through a remarkable combination of flexibility, adaptability, and intransigence. Because our Church
brings much wisdom to bear on questions ancient and new,
we Catholics need not fear any challenge that arises from society, from investigation, from wondering, even from doubt-
ing this or that approach to mission.

Questions about ministry are not new, of course. They tend to be rooted in experience and practical need. The first Christians, who gathered together in homes sharing bread and developing rituals, had to figure out how to feed the widows and impoverished members among their number. They had to structure themselves in a way that allowed them to pass on their faith to future generations (despite persecution), including evangelization throughout the Mediterranean region. Early church structures were rather fluid, the roles not uniformly defined across groups and regions. And some early callings—such as prophet, interpreter of tongues, and healer—while valid, perhaps essential for their own day, are not typical in today's parishes. As some roles took a back seat, new roles emerged.

In the fourth century, for example, thousands of laymen and women headed into the Egyptian desert to take up contemplative lifestyles that did not require ordination or structured communities. It was a particular new way of answering questions of ministry and vocation. Some were hermits, devoting themselves to prayer and fasting, not for themselves and their salvation primarily, but as an outreach for the salvation of the world. Contemplation and ascetic living was their ministry. They felt called into the desert, lured or pushed there by the Spirit—not unlike Jesus, who, before his public debut as a rabbi was led into the desert by the same Spirit. Over time, these desert mothers and fathers formed distinct communities, the forerunners of future monks and nuns.

As the institutional dimension of our Church took shape, two clear paths to ministry and a specific understanding of the word *vocation* arose. Vocation referred to a permanent state of life: priestly ordination or vowed religious life (that is, brothers and sisters in community). Ministry was what such ministers did—whether contemplative or active. The "who" (the minister) determined the "what" (ministry).

Consequently, for centuries Catholics have benefited from those who ministered in the name of the Church as "the ordained," priests and pastors on the one hand, and as "vowed religious"—missionaries, teachers, preachers, mystics, and so forth, on the other hand. These ministries continue today on a global scale, increasing in some areas while decreasing markedly in others.

The very clarity of the ministry and call to *some*, however, and the holiness attached to those two styles of vocation, caused a misconception to creep into the thinking of the Church. The great majority of Catholics, the laity, saw their ministry and vocation in rather negative terms, as *not* ministers, *not* religious, and *not* called. This thinking ran counter to Scripture, of course. Theologians did what they could to develop the idea that the "married state" or the "single state" was the layperson's "calling." Their apostolate was to be "the world." But the lay province of family and work seldom proved comparable to the motivating force of ordination or life in a religious community, nor was it considered "holy." Not, that is, if one were to judge by the number of lay saints compared with that of priests and religious.

The pyramid that imaged the Church's organizational hierarchy served double duty for centuries, reflecting not only government, but a scale of holiness as well, with most Catholics occupying last place.

While that description suffers from severe oversimplification, the basic understanding I am trying to convey has been expressed by others at different times in history. Many of the sixteenth-century Protestant Reformers, for example, while varying from one another in many ways, spoke virtually with one voice on the importance of the individual Christian, the disciple, the believer. In Luther's congregations, *every* Christian was duty-bound to read, pray over, understand, and teach the Scripture; the interpretation and study of God's revelation was open to each and all, no longer to be the province of any minority, ordained or otherwise. Similarly, in Methodist congregations, *every baptized member* was encouraged to sing with gusto, not just the trained choristers.

In the nineteenth century as Catholics immigrated to the United States, they established numerous associations in and around parishes, from the Ancient Order of the Hibernians to sodalities for women and clubs for teenagers and children. Catholic immigrant laity was not uninvolved or idle, but spent their energy overcoming hurdles of language, custom, and culture. They tended to be poor, uneducated, and unwelcome by the mainstream Protestant establishment. By contrast, the Catholic Church offered much that society denied them at first: social services, schools, and communities of worship. As their number increased, Catholics took part in novenas, the altar and rosary societies, and the Knights of Columbus. They built more parishes and schools. Twentieth-century Catholics assimilated into mainstream society and initiated their own faith-based associations, including Catholic Action, the Christian Family Movement, the Charismatic movement, the Catholic Worker, Right to Life, and many others, rallying all Catholics around questions of mission and call. By the century's end, Catholics were the largest, most affluent religious denomination in the country, a position Catholics occupy today.

In the 1960s, the bishops at the Second Vatican Council stressed "full, active participation" of the entire assembly at Mass and wrote of the lay apostolate not merely as a support for the work of the priests but as a work of their own in the world and in the Church. Such clarity led to greater engagement by lay Catholics. The Council was, after all, another effort at internal church reform, one that continues to take place.

The response of the faithful to such Catholic teaching was immediate and has proved enormously fruitful over time. Even as some Catholics began to shed their immigrant Catholic identity and embrace the individualistic freedoms of the U.S. cultural mainstream, another contrary development began to take place. The Church experienced an infusion of lay leadership, as the laity led religious education, Christian initiation, and other outreach programs, such as peer ministry for the bereaved, imprisoned, illiterate, and those needing food and shelter. The laity led prayers and communion services, social action and social justice activities, parish pastoral and finance councils, and stewardship campaigns. They ran Catholic schools, universities, and hospitals. And large numbers of Catholic laity volunteered for liturgical roles (as lector, song leader, extraordinary minister of the Eucharist, greeter/usher, altar server).

Today every parish relies on a core group of parishioners

who are skilled and willing to maintain its ministries, and sometimes to initiate new ones. Catholics involved in parishes show keen interest in Scripture, spirituality, parish life and worship, and parish governance. They are aware of the Church's role in society and are educated to assume leadership roles in parish and church, better educated than Catholics have ever been before.

As an editor for seventeen years at *Church* magazine—in the trenches with pastors and parish leaders—I have become increasingly concerned about Catholics who have become intensely involved in parish life and have internalized the participation urged by the Council Fathers.

It led to the questions that underlie the idea for this series: Is everyone who takes part in the Church's ministry a minister? What about other acts of charity and justice, such as caring for an elderly neighbor, helping to build a house through Habitat for Humanity, donating to the Red Cross—are those ministries? And what about the term *minister*? How does such language communicate, given the established, official ministers of our Church—the ordained and vowed religious? And what about two relatively new groups of people on the scene: the fifteen thousand permanent deacons who have (post–Vatican II) taken vows to serve under specific bishops, and the thirty-one thousand lay ecclesial ministers now serving in two-thirds of Catholic parishes (as directors of religious education, pastoral associates, liturgists, youth directors, and so on)? They too must be fitted into the discussion of ministers and ministry.

The timing for lay interest in things Catholic is more than auspicious. The extraordinary influx of religious and priestly vocations that began in the 1950s appears to have run its course. The number of such vocations has drastically decreased in recent years.

How imperative, then, that clergy, religious, and laity find effective ways of relating to one another. What better way to begin than by starting with the basic questions of mission, ministry, and call? In general, Catholics could benefit from a more refined understanding of the interdependence among the various "callings" of the Spirit within our Church. Is there a spirituality "of" ministry or "for" ministry that binds all these "professionalized" ministers together? Does it bind them as well to all baptized Catholics who are trying to follow Jesus as disciples? Is ministry being expanded or redefined?

In terms of spirituality—that elusive word that evokes one's prayer life and interior disposition toward God and neighbor—what prayer and practices uphold these groups or subgroups within the whole? Can one spirituality serve them all without blurring important distinctions? Or is it better to carefully forge different but related ways of coming before God, practices that fit more snugly and appropriately the work and self-understanding of each kind of minister and ministry?

We have reached another critical juncture in the road, I think. The Church's injunction to witness to the Gospel in each generation is as difficult as ever today, whether the challenge is posed by militant sects within Islam or by secularism. Recent generations have faced Fascism, Communism, and the idolization of science as religion. Will the most highly educated Catholic laity in history engage its peers and its own children and enlist them in the Church's cause? Or will it alienate them, or watch them drift away from a church they see as indifferent or irrelevant to their lives?

This set of questions I sought to explore, thinking that a solid set of writers could take the discussion a step further. I would need to find a good mix of theologians, leading Catholic laity, academics, and pastoral ministers, men and women who could write in a clear and compelling way. In collaboration with the magazine's publisher, Father Eugene Lauer, we composed an author-invitation list of seven names.

The list includes a noted pastor and campus minister (Rev. James J. Bacik); an inspirational speaker, writer, and active parishioner (Patricia H. Livingston); and several theologians spread around the nation: Dr. Doris Donnelly (Cleveland), Dr. Edward P. Hahnenberg (Cincinnati), Rev. Ronald Rolheiser, OMI (San Antonio), Dr. Michael Downey (Los Angeles), and Susan K. Wood, SCL (Milwaukee). These theologians bring substantial expertise in spirituality, lay ministry, liturgy, seminary education, and Eucharist. The list can be parsed in other valuable ways as well. It contains four laypeople (two women, two men); two persons in religious orders (one priest, one sister); and one diocesan priest. We found the spread of perspectives we originally sought.

The essays appeared originally as a series in *Church* magazine, evoking keen reader interest. Subscribers sought permission to photocopy the series or asked for a specific issue they had missed. This volume should satisfy that demand.

The insights presented here make the volume valuable. It will appeal not only to Catholic pastors, parish staff members, and active lay Catholics, but to students in seminaries and ministry education programs as well. This round of the dialogue on minister and ministry is still young. In the hands of such experienced and competent conversation partners, the book will, I hope, stimulate many more fruitful discussions among readers.

KAREN SUE SMITH
NEW YORK CITY

Contributing Authors

Rev. James J. Bacik, DPhil, is a campus minister at the University of Toledo and serves as the pastor of Corpus Christi University Parish, Toledo, Ohio.

Doris Donnelly, PhD, is professor of theology and director of The Cardinal Suenens Program in Theology and Church Life at John Carroll University in Cleveland, Ohio. She is a former president of the North American Academy of Liturgy.

Michael Downey, PhD, is the cardinal's theologian, Archdiocese of Los Angeles, and professor of systematic theology and spirituality at Saint John's Seminary, Camarillo, California. He is the author of *The Heart of Hope: Contemplating Life, Awakening Love* (Pauline, 2005). In 2005 Pope John Paul II awarded him the cross Pro Ecclesia et Pontifice.

Edward P. Hahnenberg, PhD, is assistant professor of theology at Xavier University, Cincinnati, Ohio. He is the author of *Ministries: A Relational Approach* (Crossroad, 2003) *and A Concise Guide to the Documents of Vatican II* (St. Anthony Messenger, forthcoming).

Patricia H. Livingston is an inspirational speaker and writer who has been giving workshops, conference addresses, retreats, and parish missions for more than twenty years. Her books are *Lessons of the Heart* and *This Blessed Mess* (Sorin Books, Notre Dame, Indiana).

Rev. Ronald Rolheiser, OMI, PhD, STD, a well-known author and columnist, is president of the Oblate School of Theology in San Antonio, Texas.

Karen Sue Smith is currently editorial director at *America* magazine, the Jesuit weekly. From 1990 to 2006 she was the editor of *Church*, the quarterly published by the National Pastoral Life Center in New York City where this series of articles first appeared. Before that, she worked as an associate editor at *Commonweal.*

Susan K. Wood, SCL, PhD, is professor of theology at Marquette University in Milwaukee. She is the author of *Sacramental Orders* (The Liturgical Press, 2000) and is editor of *Ordering the Baptismal Priesthood* (The Liturgical Press, 2003).

1

Spirituality for Church Ministers

James J. Bacik

The topic of ministerial spirituality engages two important contemporary movements: the remarkable interest in spiritual matters, which continues to grow in the United States, and the dramatic increase in the number of lay Catholics involved in ministry. At the beginning of the new millennium, spirituality is a lively topic in our country. Books on spiritual issues are selling well. Our secular culture drives many people to seek deeper meaning and purpose in life. Those suffering from addictions find help in the twelve-step programs, which have a spiritual component. All over the country, campus ministers serving residential campuses report large crowds of collegians participating in weekend liturgies. A growing number of business leaders recognize the importance of spirituality in the boardroom and at the work site. Leading scientists speak openly about the mysterious character of the universe. Health professionals are more aware of the healing power of prayer. More Catholics are seeking spiritual direction. Our noisy, fast-paced way of life is creating a thirst for quiet prayer and reflection. The still unfolding transition from the modern to the postmodern world, which touches all aspects of American life, is intensifying the quest for stability and security. Shaken by the ongoing threat of terrorism, many citizens are experiencing a new sense of vulnerability and a deeper dependence on a higher power. The pluralism, now so evident in the Catholic Church, is contributing to a new concern about Catholic identity and its spiritual core. In sum, the current interest in ministerial spirituality is part of a broad spiritual awakening in the United States.

Church Ministry

The Second Vatican Council's emphasis on the role of the laity in the Church and the world has entered the consciousness of many Catholics. The declaration "We are the church" is often heard among laypersons who feel a sense of responsibility for the well-being of their parishes and expect to have a voice in how they function. A growing number of parishioners recognize their responsibility to build up the Body of Christ and spread the reign of God in the world. Some of these dedicated people have taken on official ministerial roles. Parishes formerly staffed by two or three priests, who performed most of the ministerial duties, now typically have a staff or team of persons who exercise various roles within the faith community. This situation, which evolved gradually after the Council, has created a new set of questions about the nature of ministry and the proper relationships among various ministers.

A contemporary theology of baptism provides at least a starting point for examining these questions, which are complex and require much further discussion. All the baptized are equal members of the Church and share responsibility for making it a credible sign and an effective instrument of the kingdom. Most Christians live out their baptismal vocation by applying gospel teachings and values to their life in the world. Nourished by the liturgy and private prayer, they help spread the reign of God by founding families, raising children, earning a living, humanizing the culture, and participating in civic life. They perform their Christian service as a baptismal responsibility and not simply as a participation in the mission of the hierarchy.

Some Christians are called to official ministry within the Church. Their ministry is a specification of the baptismal vocation they share with all Christians. Bishops, for example, are sacramentally ordained to exercise pastoral oversight and care for the local diocesan church. Pastors, in union with the bishop, are appointed to be servant leaders and to proclaim the word in parishes. Deacons are ordained to carry out specific ministerial tasks, often in the area of Christian service. Other baptized persons are formally chosen, trained, and commissioned to use their gifts in an official capacity to serve the Church and the world. These ministers, who enjoy a special position in the Church, exercise a wide variety of functions: for example, running religious education programs, directing youth ministry, coordinating social justice efforts, reading the Scriptures and distributing Communion at Mass, administering parishes, serving as pastoral associates, directing choirs, caring for the sick, offering spiritual direction, and visiting prisoners. Pastors today have the task of recruiting talented people, providing them with proper training, and coordinating their efforts to create a viable flourishing parish. All of these ministers are living out their baptismal vocation and are not simply helping out the pastor.

A Baptismal Spirituality

By virtue of baptism, church ministers are called to holiness and a deep spirituality, which is the wellspring of effective ministry. Like the word *health*, spirituality is hard to define in the abstract and is better understood by discussing it functionally. It points to our relationship to the mystery dimension of human existence, the transcendent realm, the ultimate reality. It turns us to the great issues of identity, meaning, purpose, and integrity. It calls for discernment, growth in virtue, effective living, and deeper relationships. The word raises important practical questions that are personally engaging, for instance: How can I remain composed in the midst of the tensions of life? What role can I play in establishing greater justice in society? How can our family avoid the seduction of consumerism?

Before discussing the specific contours of ministerial spirituality, I think it fitting and instructive to examine the spirituality common to all baptized Christians. Authentic Christian spirituality reflects our fundamental belief in trinitarian monotheism (one God, three persons).

God: Mature Christians recognize their complete dependence on the one God, traditionally addressed as Father, who is the source and goal of life and exercises maternal care on all creatures. Worship and prayerful reflection express and nourish a proper sense of dependency, which grounds all of our efforts to cooperate wholeheartedly and intelligently with God in serving the kingdom. The great theologians understood that God remains Mystery beyond all words and images. Referring to the ultimate Reality, Augustine insisted that if we understand it, then it is not God. Aquinas said that the most important thing to know about God is that we do not know God, adding that even in the beatific vision God remains the inexhaustible mystery. Karl Rahner taught that during our earthly journey we human beings remain searchers, who must accept that any and all words from God are limited and partial. Ministers guided by reflection on the mystery are less likely to speak glibly of God and to impose their own limited images of God on others.

Jesus the Christ: All Christians are called to put on the mind of Christ, to see the world through his eyes. The Word made flesh, Jesus of Nazareth, is the wisdom of the Father. Jesus is our spiritual guide. He knows the secrets of God and reveals the divine will to us. From the historical Jesus we learn respect for others, compassion for the suffering, forgiveness of enemies. His message for all disciples is to take up the cross daily and follow him.

Spiritual growth occurs as we enter more fully into the paschal mystery, the death and resurrection of the Lord. The *Kenosis* joys of ministry flow from dying to self in service to others. A Christocentric spirituality also has a prophetic edge. In Luke's Gospel, Jesus indicates that he has come to preach the good news to the poor and to liberate the captives (4:16–21). In his ministry, he broke social taboos by reaching out to women and outcasts. In Matthew's Gospel, Jesus identifies himself with the hungry and homeless and teaches that his followers will be judged on their response to those in need (25:31–46). Church ministers grow in holiness by meditating on the scriptural witness to Jesus Christ and following his example of self-sacrificing love.

The Holy Spirit: Western Christian spirituality has suffered from a lack of attention to the Holy Spirit, the forgotten person of the Trinity. This development counters the original thrust of the apostle Paul, who insisted that the Spirit guides Christians in the great struggle against all demonic forces by conforming us to Christ and endowing us with special gifts or *charisms.* Spirit-filled Christians manifest enthusiasm, spontaneity, and energy for the cause of God and humanity. In John's Gospel, Jesus promises the Paraclete to strengthen and instruct us. We have the task of cooperating with the Spirit in discerning the best ways of serving the kingdom. The gifts of the Spirit are given not for personal gain but for the common good. When the Holy Spirit is neglected, spirituality tends to become dry, rigid, and exclusive. Ministers attuned to the inner promptings of the Paraclete tend to be more open and inclusive in responding to the needs of those they serve.

Christians who take seriously their vocation to holiness come to know both the destructive force of sin and the greater power of grace. In this spiritual combat, we need virtues that incline and enable us to practice our Christian faith in complex and changing situations. Ministers who cooperate with grace by cultivating the theological virtues (faith, hope, and charity), as well as the traditional moral virtues (prudence, justice, fortitude, and temperance), make progress on the path toward greater holiness and are better prepared to preach the gospel by example and not just by words.

For all the baptized, the spiritual quest is common: union with the Father, through the incarnate Son in the power of the Holy Spirit. Ministers who recognize that they share the spiritual journey with their fellow parishioners can speak more authentically of common struggles and shared joys.

A Ministerial Spirituality

The spiritual quest, as lived experience, is both common and particular. For Christians, spirituality is essentially incarnational. We believe that individuals meet God in the concrete particularities of everyday life. The shape of discipleship is influenced by our state of life as well as the challenges and joys of our daily work. The Spirit speaks to us in and through our unique personalities and our specific struggles with the dark forces.

Public Representatives: The distinctive character of ministerial spirituality flows from the special public position of ministers within the Church. The spirituality of ministers displays a thick ecclesial texture. Those of us representing the Church often find ourselves called to explain or defend its teachings and practices. Ministers tend to spend more time pondering and discussing internal Church matters than their fellow Christians immersed in the task of spreading the kingdom in the world. In a more direct and explicit way, we carry the glories and the burdens of Church history, including the current crisis in the U.S. Church. We cannot completely ignore the disputes between official Church teaching and the dissenting opinions of the people we serve. Much of our time and energy is devoted to ecclesial challenges, such as promoting more active participation in the liturgy and finding more effective ways of passing on our Catholic tradition to the next generation. The rhythm of the Church year and the great feasts tend to structure our imaginations. We must work hard to find a style of leadership that is faithful to the Gospel and meets the needs of our fellow parishioners. For Church ministers, the path to holiness necessarily passes through the complex and absorbing domain of Church affairs.

Facing Temptations: Ministers immersed in the life of the Church are especially prey to the temptation of "ecclesiolotry," the tendency to make an idol out of the Church. At the root of this temptation is the failure to distinguish between the Church and the reign of God's justice and peace in the world. The Church is not the kingdom. It is the graced but sinful sign and instrument of the kingdom. Ministers who ignore this distinction are in danger of idolizing the Church, turning an important concern into an ultimate concern. This leads to some destructive misperceptions: that all the baptized should be as concerned about internal Church affairs as we are; that holiness is reserved for those in official Church positions; and that the task of humanizing the world must be controlled by the Church hierarchy.

In this time of unprecedented crisis for the Church in the United States, many ministers are struggling to avoid falling into a tired cynicism. The constant barrage of negative publicity over the sexual abuse scandal can wear us down. The agonized cries of victims tear at our hearts. The depressing public exposure of the misdeeds of our ministerial friends and colleagues can prompt a draining self-examination of the way we have all tarnished the image of genuine servant leadership. The zero-tolerance policy strains our ability to proclaim Christ's teaching on forgiveness. It is no wonder that many ministers are weary of it all and are struggling to remain positive about the future of the Church.

Humble Confidence, the Great Ministerial Virtue

Recognizing the temptations to ecclesiolotry and cynicism, Church ministers do well to cooperate with God's grace in cultivating the virtue of humble confidence.

First of all, we need confidence that our ministry is important and valuable. Our culture acclaims those who attain specific material goals, such as making money, achieving status, producing goods, and gaining power. The dominant culture is not good at recognizing spiritual contributions and accomplishments.

Given this materialistic bias, which affects believers as well, it is vital for Church ministers to develop an inner confidence that our work is meaningful and helpful. We represent the Catholic tradition, which has valuable resources for responding to the destructive trends in postmodern culture: a communal sense of human existence that challenges rugged individualism; a tradition of asceticism that counters consumerism; a natural-law ethic that opposes total relativism; and a rich spiritual tradition that exposes the superficiality of our materialistic culture.

Furthermore, ministers bring the Gospel to crucial moments in the lives of individuals and families, ranging from the baptism of babies through preparation for marriage, to the burial of the dead. People allow us into their lives at times of deep spiritual need. We need confidence that we are the bearers of good news.

Humility prompts us to recognize our personal limitations and our complete dependence on God. It is the power of divine grace that works in and through us to help spread the kingdom. We are ambassadors of Christ, who strengthens us for the task of sharing the Good News. The Holy Spirit can transform our weakness and limitations into instruments of healing and spiritual growth for others. We do not need to be perfect or have all the answers to minister effectively. Humility, rooted in truth, bolsters our confidence and deepens our trust in God.

A Spirituality:
Both Situational and Structured

Ministerial spirituality has a distinctive way of being both situational and structured. Our official duties and specific responsibilities within the Church can serve as fruitful situational catalysts for spiritual growth. For example, directors of religious education and catechists need to study and appropriate their Christian faith; preachers must ponder the meaning of the Scriptures for everyday life; lectors should reflect on the passages they read at Mass; couples in charge of marriage preparation have the opportunity to enrich their own marriages; social activists can deepen their commitments by reflecting on Catholic social teaching; lay ecclesial ministers need a hopeful realism to sustain them when they are misunderstood and underappreciated; music directors have the opportunity to develop an integrated liturgical piety; spiritual directors can find inspiration for their own growth from the progress of those they direct; prison chaplains need the virtue of hope in dealing with sin, weakness, and tragedy; campus ministers need a committed openness to serve today's collegians. Ministerial successes can lead to spontaneous prayers of gratitude; the failures to an honest examination of conscience; and the complex challenges to a process of discernment. Ministry writes an impressive agenda for a situational spirituality.

Spiritual growth also demands structured approaches and systematic efforts to cooperate with God's grace. Ministers have the opportunity to construct their own regimen out of the traditional sources of spiritual nourishment: liturgy,

Scripture, spiritual reading, prayer, meditation, fasting, and examination of conscience. We should determine a workable configuration of these practices, which we can actually do regularly in the midst of a busy schedule and which will enhance our ability to detect the presence of grace in diverse ministerial situations.

2

First the Dying

Patricia H. Livingston

❧

*I guess I never hear about the care we give in our
own families as if it were on a par with* ministry.

For me the bottom line is simple: I think spirituality
for ministers is, at its heart, the same as spirituality
for everyone else. Even the word *ministry* can be problematic in some ways. It seems to set aside a kind of activity
as if it were very "other." In my own life, at least, it has
not been useful to think of my "ministry" as opposed to
my other life activities. That kind of compartmentalization
can cause needless suffering, as this story about my sister Peggy and the late Bishop Kenneth Untener illustrates.

For seven years I was the associate director of a sab-
batical program at the University of Notre Dame for men
and women in full-time Church ministry. In the course of
each four-month program, we invited nearly forty different

presenters to give minicourses for the participants. One such presenter (whose sudden death I am still grieving) was Bishop Untener of Saginaw, Michigan. This particular year the thrust of his final afternoon class was ministry to the poor: the central "mission of ministry"—that every parish and organization in his diocese find ways to serve the poor. Untener described a yearlong process that required each meeting to open with the question: "How does what we are doing in this meeting serve the poor?"

My sister Peggy, who was visiting me, had gone to Untener's class. That night the priest who directed the program with me, Father Eugene F. Lauer (now director of the National Pastoral Life Center), and I took Peggy and Bishop Untener to dinner. Untener, who loved to get feedback from people, asked Peggy what she thought about his focus on ministry to the poor.

She told him she thought it was extremely important, moving, and admirable, but that it left her feeling the same way the latest thrust of the Renew program in her home parish had left her. Since this cycle of Renew focused on social justice outreach, the parish was passing around sign-up sheets asking parishioners to take a turn at a soup kitchen or homeless shelter.

"I left Mass that day the way I left your class this afternoon, Bishop," she said, "feeling guilty, inadequate and less-than."

"Why is that?" he asked, surprised, paying attention.

"Because I couldn't possibly sign up. In my family right now I am the frontline in arranging and supervising the care for five of our beloved older people. Our dad, who has

Alzheimer's; our mom, who has a form of cancer; our aunt, who has had a stroke; and two cousins of Dad's who never married and are helpless physically and mentally. Much of every weekend is spent checking on their care, visiting them, shopping for them, making sure they know they are loved. I am doing this in the midst of my job and raising my family. I cannot possibly go to a soup kitchen or a homeless shelter."

For a minute she was quiet and then continued, "I guess I never hear about the care we give in our own families as if it were on a par with 'ministry.' I am always left feeling somehow less..."

At a conference two years later, I saw Bishop Untener, who told me that Peggy's reflection was still affecting him. He said she had awakened him to a dichotomy sometimes implied in the Church between "ministry" and "ordinary life." He had begun to notice the real heroism of care that took place in family after family—for old and young, sick and struggling, the "poor" of all kinds. Untener himself had begun talking about it in homilies and conferences, and people were responding with deep gratitude.

My first point, then, is that a spirituality for ministry is no different from the spirituality of living the Christian life, as all of us are to live it.

One component of a spirituality for all of us is that it involves some kind of reaching out, giving ourselves, caring for others, whether in a formal ministerial setting or not. I do not think, however, that spirituality begins with our actions toward others. Rather, it begins with our living relationship to God in the very real moments of our lives.

What form this takes comes from the beliefs and practices, images and habits, thoughts and feelings, we have in response to God's presence as we experience it. What we all have in common is that God's presence is revealed in our everyday living. For some of us, it involves serving in an official capacity in the Church. Yet all of us must ultimately discover our radical dependence on a God who loves us in ways that take our breath away, and who stretches us far beyond what we would ever choose. That is where spirituality leads, for everyone, whatever his or her particular vocation or status in life.

Certain givens are to be expected. Everyone's journey in spirituality sooner or later involves enormous difficulty—of one type or another. None of us can help struggling against that fact, since we naturally tend to feel it is some kind of mistake. We do not like it that life inevitably involves mess.

The truth of the human condition, though, is that the pattern of our lives asks of us more than we could ever dream, emptying us until we feel we have lost all there is to lose. Then, and here is the key to all spirituality, *then*... "give, and it will be given to you [filling us a hundredfold]; good measure, pressed down, shaken together, running over..." (see Luke 6:38).

What we are all painfully challenged by, but utterly graced to experience in our lives, is that the grain of wheat has to fall to the ground and die in order to bear fruit. But bear fruit it does. And bear fruit it will.

I believe that this truth has to come home to us in a very concrete way, in some place where the rubber hits the road, before we understand that our own story is nothing less than the story of the paschal mystery itself. Again and again we must take up our cross. Again and again the cross leads to new life.

New life has repercussions for ourselves and for the way we relate to other people. One night, a priest-member of a long-standing faith-sharing group to which I belong reflected on his upcoming twenty-fifth anniversary in priesthood. He said he owed the depth of his priesthood to his brother. I was surprised. I did not remember ever hearing much about his brother, just that there were only the two of them growing up with his mom. His dad had died young.

"Because of my brother," he said, "I began my priesthood with a deep sense of connection with the lives of my parishioners. I felt one with them. And they trusted me."

"Because of your brother?" I asked, still puzzled.

He flushed a little, awkward, "Maybe I haven't told you..." He paused, took a deep breath, and continued, "I went to the seminary hundreds of miles from home. When the time came for my ordination, my brother was driving my mother out for the ceremony. On the way, one of the tires blew out on their car, it swerved into an oncoming vehicle, and my brother was killed. My mother came to the ordination in bandages. My first Mass was my brother's funeral Mass."

I sat in stunned silence with the rest of our group, tears coming down our faces.

"As strange as this sounds," he said to us gently, "that broke me open at a very deep level. People's losses and disappointments—their suffering was like my own. We are in this together, all of us. Standing in the mystery with the One who joined us on this same journey. The mystery of life from death. The mystery we call love." This, for me, is the heart of spirituality for us all.

3

The Power of Gravity: Shaping a Personal Spirituality for Ministry

Doris Donnelly

True conversion is always about invitation, not intimidation; about the movement from confusion to clarity; and about receiving, not rejecting, what we love most.

When you hear the term *ministerial spirituality*, you may wonder whether one school or style or approach to spirituality suits everyone, at least everyone who engages in a formal ministry. Is there a pattern out there that can be fitted to each one of us without alteration? Does one size fit all?

I don't think so. But like you I am also aware that there are paths and signposts along the way common to all of us.

Is there anyone among us, for example, who does not understand at some basic gut level Dante's description of the painful reconfiguration of desires in the *Purgatorio*? Or the welcome peace of the *Paradiso*? Who does not identify at least a little bit with Henri Nouwen's lifelong struggle with the need to be noticed and affirmed? Or with Dorothy Day's decision to leave her common-law husband after the birth of a daughter whom she wanted baptized to celebrate what she perceived as an undeserved but glorious gift from God?

But if one size is not the solution, how then can we find our own path, our personal custom-made way?

Gravity helps.

Gravity is the tug that attracts us to the path and often to the cause of someone who has gone before us: Francis of Assisi, Gandhi, Teresa of Calcutta, Thomas Merton, or any of countless others. For some, the gravitational pull is so great that friends, relatives, and acquaintances commit themselves lock, stock, and barrel to a spirituality mapped out by someone else. The fit seems right; they take the plunge wholeheartedly and make it a lifestyle.

Drawn to the Ignatian Way

For me, the gravitational pull came at a time and from a source that I could not have predicted. It surfaced shortly after the birth of my son when I was introduced to a Basque soldier saint, Ignatius of Loyola. As a voracious reader of their biographies from the time I was in elementary school, I knew about Ignatius and several other Jesuit saints. I was partial to stories about Jesuit missionaries like Isaac Jogues,

René Goupil, Jean de Brébeuf, Matteo Ricci, and, of course, Francis Xavier.

This more intimate introduction to Ignatius, however, came by way of a Jesuit priest who took my pious sentiments and faint yearnings for God more seriously than I did myself. Over the course of several conversations, he suggested that I consider an eight-day retreat. At the time the idea struck me as lunacy since I had a husband and an eighteen-month-old son at home and a demanding teaching post at a university. The cup of my everyday "ministries" was already overflowing. But it came to pass, and in the hands of another Jesuit priest—and Ignatius, I like to think—I made the Spiritual Exercises for the first time.

What Ignatius did was to affirm certain intuitions of mine about heaven, love, sin, commitment, prayer, and faith. Through Ignatius I heard experiences like mine *acknowledged*. At times, I became aware to the point of alarm that God could speak clearly and directly to me. In the course of just a week I was able to feel totally secure and thoroughly grateful as I'd never been before.

The eight-day Ignatian retreat is an abbreviated version of the thirty-day master plan that is more or less divided into four weeks. Each week has a defined focus that in turn elicits particular graces to be prayed for specifically. On my first retreat—and on several since then—I never budged from the "first week" and it hardly mattered. Even when the pacific euphoria was shattered by my vagrant meanderings, I never succumbed to thinking that I did not belong, that I was not at home.

As decisive as the influence of Ignatius has been for me, mine is not a formal relationship with him or the Society of Jesus. If you are thinking of the Benedictine Oblates or the Third Order Franciscans or various associate programs with religious communities—all great ideas, incidentally—my affiliation is not like those. The gravitational pull to Ignatius is something like that of a pin to a magnet—the stuff of an ordinary pilgrim with a better than ordinary appreciation of her good fortune in being in such good company.

I think the attraction to Ignatian spirituality continues for me and for many others because Ignatius understands what the process of conversion, primary and ongoing, is about. It made sense in the sixteenth century and it makes sense now, five centuries later, because Ignatius lived through it himself. He walked the walk that makes the talk so credible.

Ignatius understood that true conversion is always about invitation, not intimidation; about the movement from confusion to clarity; and about receiving, not rejecting, what we love most.

Invitation, Not Intimidation

Ignatius begins as any good psychologist (or wise father or mother or pastoral minister) does, with an invitation. Adults know that the opposite—intimidation—never really works. It threatens and frightens, but after the alarm is over nothing much changes except that we (or those we intimidate) live in a perpetual state of anxiety, dreading the next attack. Manipulating religious language with hellfire images and grotesque punishments has been a specialty in some circles but has never yielded confident, joyful disciples.

Oddly enough, Ignatius wants the same thing as the

fearmongers. He wants our attention but elicits it by inviting rather than forcing us to meet the very person (Person) responsible for our existence. He encourages us to experience intimately the unabashed and unremitting goodness of this God and allows us to be seduced and enveloped in the embrace of pure love.

Even immovable objects, such as we sometimes are, cannot resist the power of love. Nor can we miss noting our meager response to or outright dismissal of it. For Ignatius, though, there is no rush to judgment. He holds the invitation envelope open and allows time for regret, compunction, and correction to be folded into it and purified. Neglect, error, even extreme cruelty are, for Ignatius, utterly within the reach of God's boundless forgiveness and compassion.

From Confusion to Clarity

Like many spiritual guides, Ignatius assumed confusion from those he was leading on the path to God, because the journey initially involved dissolving old loyalties and pledging new ones.

What surprised Ignatius was that even after his conversion there were more refined and subtle confusions to be faced. Gravity again played a part in sorting them out. He drew from his own experience an interesting and, as it turned out, original approach, namely, that he could "test" and subsequently validate whether an experience of confusion was a good thing or a negative influence. The process of that testing has come to be known as *Ignatian discernment.* Here is an example of how it worked.

When his plans to remain in Jerusalem were aborted, Ignatius became a student and found himself absorbed in intimate prayer while lessons were going on. While the presence of Christ was both welcome and comforting, Ignatius was pulled to reflect on the certainty that it was God's will that he be in studies so that he could be better prepared to serve others. At the same time he recognized that the experiences of Christ were interfering with his studies. Strange as it might seem, he found that neglecting his studies was derailing him from what he was supposed to be doing. The bottom line for Ignatius was the ability to discern a false consolation under the guise of a true one. Not all that glistened was gold.

Transposing this insight to more mundane proportions, it is the confusion someone like me experiences when I find time to read a book in my field—or any book for that matter—that would enhance my perspective on people and the world situation when instead I ought to be grading papers—a task for which I have no soft spot. On the other hand, with all my heart I know I am a teacher, called to be teacher. Teaching is, hands down, my vocation—the place I find joy—so that no matter how much professional improvement comes from sidestepping my responsibilities to read my students' papers, I am pulled not by guilt but by gravity and grace to do what I have come to understand with a high degree of certainty is God's will for me.

Once the insight emerged for Ignatius, he promised undivided attention to his studies. For me, *le même:* grading papers turns out to be the greater good by far.

From Rejecting to Receiving

Conversion does strange things to people. Some go overboard in rejecting what went before. Think of overeaters who, after their conversion, go to the other extreme, measuring each microgram of food that touches their lips. We hear about smokers who not only give up tobacco but also feel the need to sermonize the unconverted about the health hazards of their disgusting habit.

Some religious-conversion stories relate the converts' odd and even bizarre reactions to their sinful pasts in the form of severe bodily mortifications or extreme seclusion in total repudiation of "the world" as the temptation that led them down the wrong path in the first place.

It never seemed quite right to me that we abandon the world God created and left unfinished for us to complete. After all, isn't it our baptismal responsibility to build the kingdom of God on earth? How is that going to happen if we give up on it and flee to the hills or cower in caves for the rest of our lives?

A perspective regarding the goodness of the world— while at the same time being aware of its destructive tendencies—fits hand in glove with my understanding of and affinity for Ignatius.

It is true that Ignatius went through a spell of renouncing the world—living like a vagabond with hair, nails, and clothes unkempt—but as his conversion deepened, so did his affection for the world. When Jesus said that his disciples were in the world but not of the world (see John 15:19), he could also have been speaking of Ignatius.

What appealed to me from the start was that Ignatius saw the world filled with the presence of God. Theologians call this the *sacramental principle*. As another Jesuit, Avery Dulles, put it, "Strictly speaking, there is nothing which could not, under favorable circumstances, become a symbol of the divine" ("The Symbolic Structure of Revelation" in *Theological Studies 41*, March 1980). According to this principle, God can be met in friendships, marriage, childbirth, illness, celibacy, beauty, our work—if we only have eyes to see. Ignatius was convinced (as I am) that God leaves footprints and traces everywhere. Learning to spy them, inviting attention to them, celebrating them, praying them—this is the stuff of our ministry and our life.

Ignatius was at ease in the world. He reveled in the superabundant gift of God's creation. At the same time he knew reveling was not going to be his full-time job. He knew that contemplation would need to be accompanied by an equal measure of action.

That balance strikes me as just right.

Finding your own path

It is true that one size does not fit all when it comes to the spiritual journey. Each of us is more than the roles that we assume in our life and our work. The spirituality that nourishes us should feed the whole person and not just the part that ministers. You must find the path that feels right for you, the route to which you gravitate. The story of my comfort with (and challenges on) the path that Ignatius of Loyola mapped out is surely not for everyone. For me, it remains a lovely gift of friendship not only with God but with a soldier-saint who believed that one person at a time mattered. One of those persons was a pilgrim in Cleveland, Ohio.

4

It All Begins in Baptism: Spirituality for Lay *Ecclesial* Ministry

Edward P. Hahnenberg

Without the security that comes from ordination or vows, lay ecclesial ministers articulate their vocation in dynamic, open-ended ways. It can demand of the minister a continual conversion.

In 2001 a subcommittee of the U.S. Catholic Bishops' Conference commissioned a study on the spiritual formation of lay ecclesial ministers—and the results were encouraging. Surveying the 323 lay-ministry formation programs run by dioceses, colleges, seminaries, or independent groups (of which 207 responded), the report found that seven in ten programs include some type of formal spiritual formation com-

Z an not dols thsr

ponent. This formation often includes a variety of elements: theological reflection, faith sharing, courses on spirituality, prayer, retreats, mentoring, and/or spiritual direction. On average, participants spent one-third of their time on issues of spiritual formation. And these participants already come with a healthy desire to serve others and a commitment to the person of Jesus Christ. By the time they leave, these qualities—along with a host of other positive ministerial qualities—are stronger and more fully developed. It seems that lay ministry programs are taking spiritual formation seriously, and they're doing the formation well.

But what takes place outside of these programs? With more than thirty thousand lay ecclesial ministers working in our parishes, it is time to ask: How are their spiritual lives being fed? What resources can the professional parish minister draw on to support her or his life of ministry when he or she is no longer part of the intentional environment of a formation program? What are sources for the spirituality of lay ecclesial ministers?

This article points to one source: the liturgy of baptism. I hope to identify a few themes drawn from the first rite of initiation, but not to impose them. My goal is to invite lay ecclesial ministers to ask: How does the rite of baptism—which launches the Christian life and grounds all ministry—speak to our own unique way of serving the community?

The Catechumenate and Conversion

The 1972 revised rite of Christian initiation of adults introduced the catechumenate to the post–Vatican II parish. (We might be tempted to say that the rite introduced baptism itself to the parish!) The catechumenate has roots in the early Church, when a period of moral preparation and personal reflection preceded baptism at the Easter Vigil.

The catechumenate reminds us today that baptism is a process, that life as the body of Christ is dynamic, it implies growth and conversion. Looking at the rites associated with the catechumenate, we notice a series of moments that mark a turning away from sin (exorcisms, scrutinies, the renunciation of sin prior to baptism) and a turning toward God (being marked by the sign of the cross, receiving the Gospel and the Creed, the profession of trinitarian faith).

This twofold conversion is symbolized by the anointing with the oil of catechumens, itself a polyvalent sign evoking the healing and strengthening power of God. For adult catechumens, these rituals span the weeks and months leading up to the Easter Vigil, emphasizing the ongoing nature of what is a lifelong process of conversion. For infants—the baptism of our daughter Kate is the one I most vividly remember—the catechumenate is condensed to a few, potent rituals right before the water bath of baptism. These are reminders of the continual conversion to come.

The rituals of the catechumenate speak to the minister of a formation that is not only education but real conversion and transformation. *A spirituality of conversion* begins for many lay ecclesial ministers in graduate programs when they exchange catechism certainties for the mystery that lies beneath all good theology. It begins as some take on ministry full time and recognize that such a career may never bring financial security. It begins as many accept new ways of relating to family members when so many weeknights and weekends are occupied by work.

For early Christians, becoming a catechumen often meant a radical life transition—leaving certain professions and circles of friends. For many parish ministers today, their work requires both a continual turning away from what society seems to value and a constant confrontation with change. Without the security that comes from ordination or vows, lay ecclesial ministers articulate their vocation in dynamic, open-ended ways. The flexibility and freedom of lay ecclesial ministry is one of its great gifts to the church, but it can demand of the individual minister a kind of continual conversion. This is not always a conversion from sin to grace, but an ongoing process of self-reflection and self-evaluation of one's life and direction in ministry.

A Communal Celebration

When our first daughter, Kate, was baptized, our newly arrived associate pastor, Father Neil, presided. Having recently returned from a nearly two-decade mission to East Africa, Father Neil transformed that suburban Sunday liturgy into a village event. For him, welcoming these six children into this community was the highlight of the Eucharist that day. He led parents, godparents, and the entire assembly in an unrehearsed procession around the church, calling everyone out from the pews in order to crowd around the temporary font still in place in the gathering space after Easter. Kids elbowed their way up to the water. Parents juggled babies in delicate baptismal gowns and jostled for a place near the font. Godparents burned themselves on candle wax, while grandparents strained to get photographs. Everyone pressed in to see. Kate was dipped in water and slathered with oil and passed around the congregation. The church erupted in spontaneous applause. It was a mob scene. But in this chaos of coming to Christ, one thing was clear: Kate was not in this alone.

Since the Second Vatican Council, Catholics have recovered the communal dimension of baptism. No longer does baptism focus exclusively on original sin. Today the emphasis is on welcoming this new child of God (whether four months old or forty years old) into the body of Christ. What was once an automatic and mostly private rite, hastily administered after the birth of an infant, has become a liturgical celebration shared by many. And with the revised initiation rite, the whole parish is asked to help. As a community, we walk with the catechumens and candidates through their Easter journey. The traditional requirement of a godparent or sponsor affirms what the rite proclaims: we come to Christ through others, we persevere in faith with the help of others, we need others, and others need us.

A spirituality of ministry rooted in baptism cannot ignore the fundamental fact that the minister exists and acts among others: people are the context for ministry. A *relational spirituality* encourages ministers to reflect on their level of comfort in working with others, their attitudes toward personal relationships and the necessity of appropriate boundaries, their ability to collaborate, openness to constructive criticism, and willingness to be mentored.

Ministerial relationships are not only personal, however; they are also ecclesial. Most lay ecclesial ministers serve the church community directly, thus their spirituality is shaped by the work of building up the body of Christ for its mission in the world. A relational spirituality challenges the minister to work *with* the church and not simply *for* it. Lay ecclesial ministry, by its public nature and position of leadership, entails a certain responsibility to represent the larger Church beyond the parish—not to glorify the institution, but to accept the Church's mission as one's own. This does not require a quiet acceptance of every decision coming from church leaders, but it does require an effort to understand these decisions and to present them fairly. It also requires an openness to be formed by the voices of the whole Church, and not just those in charge or those with whom one interacts daily.

Potent Symbols

The communal celebration of baptism makes use of a few potent symbols. Chief among them is water, a symbol of many things. Water cleanses, refreshes, and gives life. But it also drowns and destroys (Have we already forgotten the horrible images and stories of victims of the Asian tsunami?). At the Easter Vigil we hear several readings proclaiming the ambivalence of water. And the blessing over the font presents salvation history through this lens. We hear of the abyss at the dawn of creation, the great flood, the Red Sea, the waters of the Jordan, the fluid flowing from the side of Christ crucified, and the great commission to go and baptize the world. The prayer describes water as creative, destructive, a liberation, and an initiation. It commissions and cleanses, gives new birth and buries. Like water itself, the images in this prayer rise up and overflow, spilling out into a multiplicity of meanings.

Emphasis on any one of these images introduces a distinct spirituality. For the lay ecclesial minister, we reflect on the *spirituality of death* and *new birth* emerging from the water. Early Christian architecture gives examples of tomb-shaped and womb-shaped fonts, making a point about baptism that we sometimes miss: "Do you not know that all of us who have been baptized into Christ Jesus were baptized into his death?" (Romans 6:3). At Kate's baptism, death was far from my mind. But when we brought her home afterward to a nursery filled with storybooks, blankets, and bibs covered with the popular Noah's Ark theme, I was struck by the irony. These colorful images of cute animals, smiling happily as they march two by two, come from a story drenched in death and destruction.

The force of a flood suggests a spirituality of death, speaking to all those daily deaths the minister experiences and walks through with others. Lay ecclesial ministers are not immune to disappointment—projects that fail, mistakes that are made, relationships that fall apart, frustration with fellow ministers or the people they serve. Added to this is the pain that comes to many lay ecclesial ministers—particularly women—who do not feel appreciated or recognized by the Church. Yet the Christian claim is that death is not the end. A spirituality of death and new birth points through disappointment to new directions, through failures to new ideas, through one's own pain to a presence for others in their pain.

A series of symbols and explanatory rites follows the water bath. Central is the postbaptismal anointing with chrism (which becomes confirmation in the rite of initiation for adults). Chrism is a perfumed oil that was used in the Hebrew Scriptures to anoint kings, prophets, and priests, marking them as sacred. Today the same chrism oil is used at baptism, confirmation, and the ordination of priests and bishops—making the point that we are all sacred sharers in the one priesthood of Christ, the chrismed one. We are "a chosen race, a royal priesthood, a holy nation, God's own people" (1 Peter 2:9). At our parish, the white garment (which accompanies the lighted candle in the postbaptismal rites) is shaped like a stole, symbolizing again this entrance into the priesthood of all believers. And at the Easter Vigil, everyone in the parish, not only the people to be baptized, brings a baptismal stole to wear. For the children and young adults, it is the same stole they wore at their own baptism. For older members, the stoles were prepared during Lent, often sewn together from aging baptismal gowns.

In these postbaptismal rituals a *priestly spirituality* emerges. This is not a spirituality just for the ordained, but for all the baptized. To call all of the baptized a priesthood is not to imagine the laity as "little priests" trying to imitate the ordained in a limited way. Rather, the priesthood of all believers suggests a community of people striving to live out the example of Christ's own priesthood. According to the Letter to the Hebrews, Christ's priesthood was simply his life, lived as a total response to God. His death was the sacrifice that summarized this lifelong gift of himself. And in the gospels we see that Jesus accomplished this through ministry. He preached, taught, healed, fed poor people, welcomed sinners, and confronted the unjust. These concrete images of Jesus' activity inspire lay ecclesial ministers in their many ministries: training catechists and coordinating liturgies, visiting sick parishioners in hospitals and old people alone at home, building up food pantries and organizing service trips for the youth group, listening to grieving individuals who stop by the office, and spurring comfortable parishioners to think beyond their immediate families to a world sorely in need of justice and peace. Through these activities, the lay ecclesial minister lives out and serves the priesthood of all the faithful.

Mystagogy

The rite of Christian initiation of adults does not end with baptism. It continues into the period of mystagogy, a time of postbaptismal catechesis. Today mystagogy focuses on incorporating the newly baptized into the life of the parish. But it is a process modeled on an ancient practice. From our perspective, the early Church approached sacramental preparation backward. We try to educate children and adults *before* sacramental experiences like first Communion, confirmation, or marriage. For the early Church, *the rite came first*; reflecting on the rite came after. The great mystagogical homilies of Cyril of Jerusalem, Theodore of Mopsuestia, John Chrysostom, and Ambrose are beautiful words spoken to new Christians in the weeks after their baptism. These preachers explained the sacramental mysteries that they had already experienced and named the grace that they had already received.

Theologian Richard Gaillardetz speaks of the minister as mystagogue. He notes that one of the mistakes we make in ministry is to assume that we bring God to people. That is not in fact the minister's job. For God beats us there. Every human being, from the very beginning of his or her existence, has already been touched by the presence of God. This presence may be hidden or confused or consciously rejected, but the offer of love always remains. Thus, the minister's job is to point out the grace already and always everywhere in the lives of people.

Ministers act as mystagogues by helping others to discover and understand what they have already received, but may fail to notice. A mystagogical spirituality empowers lay ecclesial ministers to name the grace in life, as well as to challenge the ways in which people obstruct God's gift. In the context of family life and parish staff, neighborhood and diocese, the lay ecclesial minister has a special role to play in witnessing to God's presence in the world. When Vatican II called the layperson "secular," it did not oppose this to the "sacred." Such would be a false dichotomy in our world of grace. By affirming the secularity of the laity, Vatican II emphasized that relationship with Christ is possible precisely in and through the ambiguity of life in the world. Lay ecclesial ministers know that this is where life in the Spirit is lived.

Conclusion

Christianity has never demanded a single spirituality for all believers. Nor can we imagine a single spirituality for all ministers, even for all lay ecclesial ministers. Any "spirituality for ministry" will always be conditioned by both a particular role and the individual person. But we all swim in the same stream whose source is Christ. And we can draw from the waters of baptism a few themes for reflection, asking how this ritual speaks to me and my unique, unrepeatable way of living a life of service in the Spirit.

5

Five Moves
for the Long Haul

Ronald Rolheiser

*The biggest danger in ministry is not so much that
we will burn out, but that we will be too self-concerned and too self-protective to live the vulnerability that lies at the heart of Jesus' ministry.*

Daniel Berrigan once wrote a little handbook on social
justice entitled *Commandments for the Long Haul*.
What an apt title! It speaks both of being practical and of
the fact that ministry is a marathon, not a short sprint. I have
chosen a similar title for these reflections, also intended to be
practical and to take seriously that ministry is marathon. A
healthy spirituality of ministry asks us to shape our energies
in a particular way and to sustain them over a long period.
Rather than using the word *commandments*, I suggest five

movements, invitations really, toward the kind of ongoing conversion needed to do ministry in Jesus' name. Each constitutes a lifelong journey, an ideal, a place where we want to be. What are these invitations? Looking at the person and ministry of Jesus, we see that to do ministry in his name, we are invited daily to move ahead in five particular ways.

1. Move from self-concern to being "food for the life of the world." What's meant by this? Recently I heard an interview with the bishop of a large diocese. At one point he was asked, "As a leader in the Church today, what do you consider as your single most important task?" The bishop, a sincere and prayerful man, answered: "To protect the faith."

I once heard England's Basil Cardinal Hume give a very different answer to the same question. Asked by a journalist what he considered to be the most important task facing the Church today, he replied, "To help save the planet."

The two are very different answers and I think we know which runs closer to Jesus.

Jesus, in defining his meaning and ministry, said, "My flesh is food for the life of the world." We can easily miss what's contained in that. Notice that Jesus is not saying his flesh is food for the minister or for the life of the Church. His body is food for the life of the world and the world is larger than the minister or the Church. Jesus came into the world to be eaten up by the world. No accident that he was born in a manger, a feeding trough, a place where animals come to eat.

We need to keep that horizon in front of us always as we do ministry. The biggest danger in ministry is not so much that we will burn out, but that we will be too self-concerned and too self-protective to live the vulnerability that lies at the heart of Jesus' ministry. A minister is meant to be vulnerable, vulnerable enough to let himself or herself be wounded, taken for granted, and ultimately "eaten up" by the needs of the world. If we do not constantly remind ourselves of that, our ministry very easily becomes a matter of feeding ourselves, looking good to others, having success in numbers, or creating safe little enclaves against the world.

We are invited to minister beyond our need to prove ourselves. An artist once shared with me what he considered the stages of growth in a good performing artist: "When you first sing live," he said, "you can't help it, but you end up making love to yourself. Eventually you progress to the point where you're making love to your audience. But you're only a real artist once you start making love to the *song!*"

Ministry, in a way, follows that pattern. When we first start out, we cannot help needing to prove ourselves, to prove that we are good at this. We might even be doing well, but, in the end, what we are doing is more about looking good than about God or about those to whom we are ministering. Eventually, we become more secure in ourselves and our focus shifts toward those to whom we are ministering. That is progress. Ultimately, however, we become really effective only when our focus is God. It is then that we can let ourselves be vulnerable, and it is then that we begin "making love to the song!"

Granted, it is not easy to get there. Yet it is only at those times when our focus is not on ourselves, nor even so much on our congregations, but on God that we move from being self-protective (and self-promoting) to being "food for the life of the world." A good spirituality of ministry challenges us to move from feeding and protecting ourselves to feeding and protecting the world.

2. Move from needing to be right to being concerned with building community. Some years ago, when I was the dean of theology at a college seminary, I received a phone call from a local pastor. Our conversation ran something like this:

"Are you the dean of theology at the seminary?" he asked.

"Yes," I replied.

"Well, I thought I'd let you know that your students are a pain in the posterior! They go to the seminary, take a couple of courses, then come back to their local communities and terrorize everyone with what they know. Nothing's ever good enough for them again, whether it's our preaching or our theology. I don't doubt they're right, but don't you teach them any compassion?"

His comments underscore a key aspect of ministry—that being right is not the only important thing. As ministers we are, biblically, "shepherds," pastors, men and women who are trying to build community. In that task, the right truth is not enough. We need the right energy and the right heart too. We can be brilliant, right, and still dysfunctional and hurtful. A good spirituality of ministry invites us to move beyond our need to be right. It tells us "to speak our truth in parables" so that, like Jesus, we can radiate a compassion and understanding that is wide enough to also embrace those who are different, wounded, ecclesially illiterate, politically incorrect, or in any other way unable to walk the road as it is mapped out in our favorite seminary textbooks.

Part of this compassion includes a willingness to bracket, when necessary, our own temperaments, ideologies, and ecclesiologies (both liberal and conservative) in order to have a compassion that, like that of Jesus, is beyond the selective sympathies of both the right and the left. It also means moving beyond the need to be successful, the need to put our own stamp on things, to leave a legacy, and to be recognized as brilliant. Fidelity, not necessarily success, is what ministry asks of us. A healthy spirituality of ministry is concerned first about the building up of community, and only afterward about having things go its own way.

3. Move from the pursuit of career and comfort to solidarity with the poor. Someone once said, "Nobody gets to heaven without a letter of reference from the poor!" That is true for effective ministry as well. Nobody is an effective minister, at least not in Jesus' name, without a real connection to the poor. That is not easy to do. We all struggle with it. We have a deep, valid need for comfort and for the kind of meaning that comes from having a successful career. Granted, we define ministry as a "vocation" as opposed to a "career," but the difference, while clear in theory, is less clear in real life. Something inside us wants to climb rather than descend (in the manner of the self-emptying of Christ). When we are honest, we have to admit that many times our own career, not the needs of the poor, is the energy driving our ministry.

It is not easy either to be in solidarity with the poor or to speak prophetically on their behalf, particularly in a culture where affluence and comfort are the most powerful narcotic ever developed. Our culture and our seminary training invite us to write the poor into our curriculum vitae, to be seen as concerned about them; but, in the end, appearance seems more important than reality here. Governments, universities, churches, and ministry, despite constant claims to the contrary, let the poor fall through the cracks, as the ever-widening gap between the poor and the rich illustrates.

Why is this? There are many reasons, but, in the end, the poor stand in the way of comfort and career. So daily, in ministry, we must recognize that we stand before the poor in a biblical fashion; namely, they are for us the person of Christ. Their exclusion is the place, always, where the cross of Christ is being erected. Nobody does real ministry in Jesus' name without a letter of reference from the poor, who stand before us always as a biblical invitation to "cross over" as Jesus did.

4. Move from the tyranny of orthodoxy, program, and cause to the compassion and prudence of Christ. In the gospels we see a very enlightening incident in Jesus' ministry. Jesus, the gospels tell us, was walking along the borders of Samaria one day when he was confronted by a Syro-Phoenician woman. The woman, a non-Jew, asks him to come and cure her daughter who is ill. Jesus initially refuses, answering her with a line that on the surface is somewhat disconcerting: "No, it is not fair to take the food of the children [the Jews] and give it to the house-dogs [the

Gentiles]!" The woman, however, shows a resilience and a shrewdness that catch Jesus flat-footed: "Ah, yes, Lord, but even the house-dogs eat the crumbs that fall off the children's table!" Jesus is so impressed that he grants her the healing.

Allow me an analogy to explain what happened. Imagine this: You are a minister in charge of running the parish program that prepares people for baptism. For a period of some months you have been preparing a dozen people. It is now just one hour before those baptisms are to take place when a woman you have never seen before approaches you and says, "I'd like to be baptized here today with these others!" I suspect that your initial reaction would be much like Jesus': "No, it's not fair to those others. You never took the program!" (The Jews had, in a manner of speaking, taken a thousand-year-long baptismal program, and Jesus was referring to it when he told the Syro-Phoenician woman that it is unfair to give the bread of the children to the house-dogs.)

If, like Jesus, you talked to her further, however, and found out that even though she had not taken the program, she was actually more ready for baptism than those who had taken it, you might, like Jesus, give her what she requested.

What this incident illustrates is that, while right program, right doctrine, right liturgy, and right preparation are important, they may never become tyrants. Jesus illustrates here, and invites us to imitate, a compassion and prudence that lie beyond program and doctrine.

History, both old and recent, shows that all of us struggle with this. Invariably some form of "legalism" (some kind of concern for boundaries, doctrine, and program, however right and valid in themselves) mitigates the compassion and prudence of Jesus.

The expression, perhaps glib today through overuse, that would have us in every situation ask, "What would Jesus do?" starts with the right question for every minister. The tension that Jesus felt in his conversation with the Syro-Phoenician woman (the tension between compassion and the hesitation that is dictated by concern for one's tradition) shows us that it is not always easy to answer that question.

Still, the invitation is always there. The compassion and prudence of Jesus beckon us beyond any tyranny that comes from orthodoxy, program, tradition, and cause. A healthy spirituality of ministry is conscious always when a minister is forever standing between the compassion of Jesus and the concern for doctrine and sound pastoral practice, but is invited, always, like Jesus, to be not legalistic or stingy with God's grace.

5. Move from compensation to affective prayer. Several years ago, I attended a retreat. Most of us arrived looking for something novel, at the cutting-edge, outside the box, something complex, but what was offered was stunningly simple. Our director spent the whole time trying to teach us how to pray in an affective way.

What exactly does that mean, to pray affectively? In essence, what our director told us might be summarized in this way: "You must learn to pray so that, in your prayer, you open yourself in such a way that sometime—perhaps not today, but sometime—you are able to hear God say to you, 'I love you!' These words, addressed to you by God, are the most important words you will ever hear because, before you hear them, nothing is ever completely right with you, but, after you hear them, something very deep will be right in your life."

John's Gospel already makes the point: the first words out of Jesus' mouth are a question: "What are you looking for?" That question remains throughout the rest of the gospel as a hermeneutical coloring suggesting that beneath everything else a certain search constantly goes on. A lot of things are happening on the surface, but underneath remains always the nagging, restless question: "What are you looking for?" Jesus answers that question explicitly only at the end of the gospel, on the morning of the Resurrection.

Mary Magdala comes looking for Jesus, but she does not recognize him. Bewildered, but sincere, she asks Jesus where she might find him (something, I suspect, we do in prayer quite a lot). Jesus, for his part, repeats for her the question with which John opens his gospel, "What are you looking for?" Then he answers it.

With deep affection, he warmly pronounces her name, "Mary." In doing that, he tells her what she and all the rest of us are forever looking for: God's voice, one to one, speaking unconditional love, gently saying our names. That is what gives us substance, identity, and justification beyond our own efforts to make ourselves lovable, worthwhile, and immortal. We are forever in fear of our own seeming insubstantiality. We need to hear God, affectionately, one to one, pronounce our names: "Carolyn!" "Julia!" "Kevin!" "Steve!" "Sophia!" Nothing will heal us more of restlessness, bitterness, and insecurity than to hear God say, *"I love you!"* That is also the key to ministry.

Jesus began his ministry only after, in his baptism, he had heard God say to him, "You are my beloved child, in whom I am well pleased!" Those words became the fuel for his ministry. The right energy for ministry is predicated precisely on hearing those words from God. When we try to do ministry on any other basis, invariably our ministry becomes compensatory, something we are doing in order to find meaning for ourselves. Unconsciously then, we begin to seek our own justification rather than letting God give us substance and we end up, as T. S. Eliot says, "doing the right thing for the wrong reason."

A life-giving, sustaining spirituality of ministry needs to remind us daily that what we are really looking for is to hear God pronounce our name in love. In the end, that is the only real fuel for ministry. Only when we affectively know God's love will we no longer feel the need to prove ourselves. Only then will we be able to make ourselves vulnerable and begin to "make love to the song!"

6

Participating in the Mission of Word and Spirit

Michael Downey

If local churches are to realize the mission of the Church, new ways forward must be found. We must discern new modes of ministry, particularly the ministry of leadership, based on charism. We cannot look only to the ordained for leadership in community.

Christian spirituality means being conformed to the person of Christ, brought into communion with God and others through the gift of the Spirit.

Cameo **Ecuador is rich in bananas.** Gathering them for export is how the people earn their livelihood in the barrios near Esmeraldas, in the Western lowlands near the sea. In the evenings, they gather for faith sharing, reflection on Scripture. A priest had been assigned to provide a sacramental ministry to these small communities, traveling from one to the next. After fifteen months, the people pooled their resources from what little they had and gave their monies to the priest, saying: We want you to go to Rome, or to Spain, or to the United States to learn how to help us understand the message of Jesus. We are not able to go away—bananas to harvest, mouths to feed, homes to tend. But you have the luxury, the freedom, and the ability to go and study. Go, then, because you are of no use to us as you are.

Cameo **Wanted: Parish Life Director.** The successful applicant will have a firm knowledge of Scripture, solid theological background, catechetical and homiletic training, and a keen sense of the needs of the local church. The search committee is seeking one who is able to lead community prayer, identify priorities and needs of the people of the parish, and oversee its liturgical life and social outreach. Above all, the ideal candidate will be able to coordinate the many gifts and ministries at Saint Leo, a growing, flourishing multicultural community of faith. Mature bilingual or multilingual men and women with rich life experience from diverse cultural backgrounds are encouraged to apply.

As these cameos show, in two very different sets of circumstances, the Church is growing in its understanding of ministry as a participatory exercise. It is the nature of the body of Christ to be blessed with many gifts, ministries, and offices. As a Christian community of faith, hope, and love, all of the baptized are called to share a common mission to proclaim and to serve the coming reign of God.

Whatever our calling, it is in service of our common call given as gift in baptism. The one call is to share in the mission of the Word and the Spirit.

If local churches are to realize the twofold mission—of the Word and of the Spirit—then new ways forward must be found. This requires discerning new modes of ministry, particularly the ministry of leadership, based on charism. We cannot look only to the ordained for leadership in community. The future entails reshaping ministerial structures to realize more effectively such a vision of mission and ministry. But the reshaping of ministerial structures will be wrong-headed if it is undertaken simply to assure that the job of running parishes and providing for sacramental needs will continue. Any reshaping of ministerial structures must be grounded in a broadly based understanding of baptismal spirituality. Such an understanding brings a fresh approach to the exercise of ministry in the Church.

In this brief article, I

- Articulate a broadly based view of baptismal spirituality
- Spell out a fresh view of ministry as a share in the mission of Word and Spirit
- Describe ministry as a participation in the life of the Trinity

- Indicate spiritual practices that help cultivate, nurture, and sustain this ministerial spirituality so that the life of the minister becomes a doxology.

Spirituality Rooted in Baptism

Even within a specifically Catholic context, *spirituality* is rather slippery, a word thickly layered with significance. I understand spirituality to refer not simply to one dimension of the Christian life, such as prayer, recollection, discernment, or ascetic practice, but to the whole of one's life. Christian spirituality means being conformed to the person of Christ, brought into communion with God and others through the gift of the Spirit.

Christian spirituality is a Trinitarian spirituality into which we are initiated by baptism. Any effort to distinguish various types of spirituality, be it that of the priest, the vowed religious, the married, the single, the deacon, the Benedictine, the Sister of Charity, or the Jesuit, must attend to distinctions only after recognizing what each has in common with all the others who—member for member—make up the Body of Christ.

In times of great transition or of perceived crisis, some groups tend to safeguard and strengthen identity—personal, corporate, or national—by way of contrast to the other, or others. In the Church, too, there are efforts to strengthen the distinctiveness of this or that church ministry, ordained or non-ordained. One hears warnings against the "clericalization of the laity" and the "laicization of the clergy."

Many forms of ministry today are rooted in secular models of leadership, with their penchant for "doing," "skills," and "outcomes," and are insufficiently informed by the riches of our theological and spiritual traditions. In contemporary understandings, there is a rather narrow focus on what one does. Faced with what is thought to be a blurring of the clergy/lay distinction, the ordained are often left wondering about their proper place in the sacramental rites, what they and only they can do, while lay ministers, or lay ecclesial ministers, often blessed with gifts of leadership and service, seek to identify the skills proper to the exercise of the ministry proper to them.

These two governing concerns—identity by contrast to the others and the focus on ministerial skills—blur the common foundations for ministry within baptism. A broadly based understanding of spirituality for ministry is urgently needed. Such a broadly based understanding of ministry rooted in baptism rests on an appreciation of the gift of God's love communicated in Word and Spirit.

The Mission of Word and Spirit

"God is love" (1 John 4:8). What is love? Love is the life that pours itself out. As gift. The gift of God's life, which is love, is constantly, everywhere and always, even in this time and place, here and now, pouring out as gift.

The Word is God's love made visible, tangible, audible. Word is God's love seen, touched, heard. Our call, that of every one of us, is to render love visible, tangible, audible, so that God is seen and touched and heard in a broken world.

Our one call is to cultivate, nurture, and sustain all manifestations of love—through preaching, teaching, the works of mercy, and through art and literature, too. In all those activities by which we contribute to love's increase in our own time and place, we are participating in the mission of the Word. The *Spirit* is God's love creating, animating, bonding. Spirit is God's very life toward us, for us, with us, and within us. Our call is to participate in all creative, animating, bonding, uniting expressions of divine love, becoming a sign of reconciliation and peace. By the gift of the Spirit, God dwells within us and gives us again and again firm faith to walk in the light of Christ, abundant hope to move forward in the face of every obstacle, and love's flourishing so that we might share in the divine life—now.

The Spirit has been given in baptism, and sealed and strengthened in confirmation. The Spirit's fruits are identifiable: love, joy, peace, patience, kindness, generosity, faithfulness, gentleness, self-control. After listing these fruits, Saint Paul reminds us that against these there is no law. How do we develop the fruits of the Spirit in the quotidian moments of our lives? How do we live together in these dark days, participating in the mission of Word and Spirit, becoming a sign of reconciliation and peace?

We must take stock of the responsibilities and the rights that are ours by baptism. The charism of leadership in the Church today entails taking baptism with utmost seriousness, calling forth the gifts of all the baptized—cultivating, nurturing, sustaining a baptismal spirituality that understands ministry as explicitly Trinitarian in its origins *and* exercise.

Ministry in Relation to the Trinity

What are the implications of a baptismal spirituality for our understanding of ministry? We begin by seeing the church as a communion. Just as Father, Son, and Spirit exist in communion and do not exist apart from their relations, so the Church is a communion of persons in relation who all together make up the body of Christ.

This means that there are no pockets of power or arenas of authority above or apart from the relations that exist between and among persons in the Church. All ministry in the Church is to be understood and exercised relationally. Deacons, priests, and bishops are not understood as some separate storehouse of sacramental power received at ordination, but, rather, in terms of a specific sacramental relationship that their ordination establishes between them and the other members of the Church. All Christian ministry, whether of the theologian, the catechist, the director of liturgy, or the ministers of hospitality, for instance, is understood in terms of the relationship of the members of the Church to one another.

The Church teaches that the Father, Son, and Spirit are different from one another, yet equal. The Father is not the Son, the Son is not the Spirit, the Spirit is neither Son nor Father, but no one of the three is less than the others. Likewise in ministry, there are different relations but none is inferior or superior to another. Grounded in the Trinity as their origin and end, various ministries and different relationships exist within the Church, each with its own activities and areas of responsibilities. But this difference does not mean that one person or ministry is greater or lesser or more easily dispensable to the life of the community. In baptism all are incorporated into the body. Each member is given a share in the mission of Word and Spirit.

Among Father, Son, and Spirit, there is an *interpenetration* (Greek *perichoresis*), a giving and receiving. This interpenetration among the three is also true of their relationship to the world and the Church. The mission of the Word is the mission of the Spirit. There is no "war of wills" between them. Within the life of the Church, too, all relationships are to be mutual and reciprocal. This is true in the parish of the lector and leader, catechist and deacon, youth director and hospital visitor. It is likewise true of bishop, priests, deacons, religious, and laypersons.

A truly baptismal spirituality, rooted in the Trinity, sees ministry as service to a community. That service is defined by mutual and reciprocal interaction—a give and take, ebb and flow, to and fro—among the various gifts with which the community has been endowed. Collaborative ministry is not merely desirable, a sort of stopgap measure in light of the diminishing number of clergy and vowed religious. Rather, it is required if the Church is to be an icon of the Trinity. The Church is true to its very nature when it calls for the full flourishing of gifts. When all the members of the body understand that they are called to participate in the mission of Word and Spirit, they will see that the quality of their interaction with one another (and those beyond their local community) is what brings divine life into the world. It matters little what is their particular job or role in the parish or diocese.

Ministry as Doxology

If one's understanding of ministry rests on the notion of being "set apart" for service, then spirituality is strengthened by accenting one's difference from others as expressed in an alternative way of life. Many seminaries reinforce such a view, signaled by geographical isolation and certain habits and dispositions fostered as "priestly formation."

If, by contrast, one's understanding of ministry is informed by pragmatic concerns, on what this or that minister does in the Christian community, then the governing concern will be with skills training.

If one's view of ministry is more broadly based, expressed in relations by which we are plunged deeply into the very life of God, then the governing concern will be to glorify God through encouraging a fuller participation in the mission of the Word and Spirit on the part of all the baptized. This is ministry as doxology.

How is a spirituality to support this view encouraged? By our being steeped in Scripture, strengthened in sacrament, and committed to being a part of God's people. Taking seriously these elements of a baptismal spirituality is a requirement, if we are to be ready for the Spirit's flourishing in our midst.

Steeped in Scripture: With the renewal of Church life and practice prompted by the Second Vatican Council, Catholics have grown profoundly in their appreciation of Scripture. Nevertheless, many still tend to think of Scripture as secondary to the sacraments. A ministerial spirituality requires that we be caught up in the rhythms of the liturgical cycle of readings. But more is asked. Day by day we need to be bathed in God's word. This requires time, if only five minutes in the morning, for sacred reading—a slow, careful pondering of God's word in the Bible.

The ancient practice of *lectio divina*, sacred reading, is a method for prayerful reading and a guide to living. It is a means of descending to the level of the heart and finding God through the simple act of reading. Binding prayer to Scripture prepares us for contemplation—being attentive to God's presence in the events of the day. In this approach, we select one line, or one word, and come back to it over and over again. We let the word "drop down" deep within us. Often without our effort, we find that it comes back to us and embraces us.

We must make time to do this. Perhaps time management is the asceticism most needed by those in Church ministry. So many of us travel through life at breakneck speed. Yet we have more time than we think: a long commute, hours spent waiting, periods standing in lines. Do we become impatient or spend such moments thanking God for the love dwelling in our hearts? What music do we listen to in the car—a cacophony that rattles the nerves or something more contemplative?

Sacred reading helps us to receive God's love as the life that constantly pours itself out. But "receiving" takes discipline. We must learn how to hear God, to receive, before we respond.

If there is one disposition to be developed by Church ministers it is *active receptivity*. It is far more important than identifying one's role in the liturgical assembly or in contrast to other ministries. The single most important vocational question is: What have I been given so that I can pass it on? To answer, we must first learn how to receive. Then, having received, we must live freely and responsibly with, in, and from the gift.

Strengthened in sacrament: In the sacraments we Christians express and receive our identity as the body of Christ in a particular time and place. We express how we hope to make good on the one and only life we have to live, and we receive the gift of God's life, which enables us to live in such a way.

For Christians, the Trinity is no mere abstraction or idea. The Trinity is acting in the community that bears Christ's name when it gathers. We are only able to come together at the font and table, for instance, because the Spirit in our hearts opens our lips to praise God. All Christian life and prayer is Trinitarian, "to the Father through the Son in the Spirit."

In the waters of baptism, by the anointing in the Spirit at confirmation, and through the ongoing celebration of the Eucharist, we are brought into a life of praise and service. We are given the grace to build a world of rightly ordered relationships rooted in equality, mutuality, and reciprocity. In the Eucharist, all who gather at the Lord's table express their willingness to work toward equality in human relationships and to build a world in which all may grow.

Hence, the question for Church ministers is not "What

am I to do in the church and do I have the skills to do it?" Rather it is: "Is doxology really at the center of my life and do I understand ministry as rooted in a baptismal, Trinitarian spirituality?" Otherwise, ministry risks bordering on pastoral malpractice. Do I see doxology and ministry (praise and service) as ways of being and building the body of Christ? A life rooted in the Trinity entails living what we say and do in liturgy, understanding ourselves as being *a part of* God's people, not set apart from them.

Committed to being a part of God's people: Finally, as the baptized we are part of and responsible for the body. All, not just some, are called to live the fullness of the Christian life through witness, worship, and service. This is our common call. Fundamentally, our Christian call is to strengthen the people of God in order to share in the mission of Word and Spirit.

We witness in many ways: by teaching, catechizing, proclaiming the word, prophetic utterance, faithfulness in illness, challenging structures and systems that depersonalize and dehumanize, constant prayer, hoping when there seems to be no reason to hope. In such ways we testify to the God who is love, life, and light.

We worship not only through full, conscious, and active participation in the sacraments of the Church but also through other activities in our lives by which God is praised and glorified. And we serve in ways both great and small, inclusive of simple acts of attending to the material needs of our families, neighborhoods, and communities, for example.

Whatever the call, whatever the gift, it is to be shared for the purpose of witness, worship, and service. In these ways the mission of Word and Spirit is realized in our own time and place.

7

Spirituality:
Diverse Paths,
Common Themes

Susan K. Wood

E ven though books with "spirituality" in the title continue
to be a hot item in bookstores, there is probably no more
difficult task than attempting to define what *spirituality* is or
to describe it, much less than to map out a spirituality for a
specific population such as lay ministers. The fact that we keep
reading essays and buying books tells me that we are always
beginning again in the spiritual life and looking for help on that
journey. No one essay or book provides the definitive recipe.

The six essays in this series, written by well-known
spiritual writers, lecturers, and theologians, have different
starting points and underlying presuppositions. The focus for
each is primarily lay ministry. Deep questions underlie these

reflections: Is a spirituality specific enough for lay ministers different from the spirituality of all Christians? How does a spirituality of lay ministers differ from a spirituality for the ordained? Aside from a minister's place in the Church, is spirituality something between myself and God—individual and private—or does it have a communal dimension? How is spirituality, so often associated with private prayer, related to the public prayer of the Church, particularly in its sacramental life? How is spirituality related to the work of the minister in the Church? How is it related to the world?

Doris Donnelly describes the Ignatian process of conversion and discernment, acknowledging that "one size does not fit all when it comes to the spiritual journey." She appreciates Ignatian spirituality because through it she was able to discern the "gravitational pull" of her vocation to be a teacher as God's will for her. She discerns God's will by listening to her deepest desires and observing where she finds joy, a joy not incompatible with having no soft spot for grading papers! She then evaluates and prioritizes her activities in the light of that core identity. In the light of this discernment grading papers rather than reading a book becomes the greater good in the light of God's call.

I suspect that that is a relative rather than an absolute priority. All teachers and ministers need to retreat from the demands of the moment and short-term goals in order to deepen their knowledge and broaden their perspective. A teacher who does not take time to read would not remain a good teacher for long. The choice between two goods is not either/or, between this desire and that duty, but a more complex one weighing time, deadlines, and multiple responsibilities. Even though Ignatius realized that the consolations of contemplation were a false consolation because they interfered with his studies, the real issue was balance between prayer and study. Ignatian spirituality enables Donnelly to order her ministerial life. It also enables her to look for the footprints and traces of the presence of God in all the events of life.

Patricia Livingston, like Doris Donnelly, does not describe a spirituality specifically for ministers. Quite the contrary. She is convinced that "spirituality for a minister is no different from the spirituality of living the Christian life, as all of us are to live it." This pattern of Christian living is the paschal mystery, the pattern of dying and rising to new life in imitation of Jesus Christ. Reading the latest spirituality book did not teach Livingston this, but the moving personal testimony of her sister Peggy, who could not volunteer for ministry because of self-sacrificing service to various family members with Alzheimer's, cancer, disability, and stroke.

Similarly, Livingston relates the story of a priest who owed his deep sense of connection with his parishioners to his experience of the death of his brother, whose funeral was this priest's first Mass. The pattern of suffering with and for another and the inevitable difficulties encountered in one's spiritual journey are common to all. Livingston is right on target in noticing that what Christians share in common is much greater than what distinguishes us in our ministerial positions or states of life within the Church. These differences melt away before the self-sacrifice demanded of each of us in the face of another's need or pain.

Nevertheless, we do need to distinguish between

Christian discipleship—sometimes mistaken for ministry—and *ecclesial* ministry, that is, ministry in the name of the Church. Patricia Livingston notes that "the word *ministry* can be problematic" because it compartmentalizes "ministry" as opposed to her other, more ordinary life. Her baptismal life is compartmentalized from her ministerial life. This presupposes that there is no difference between Christian discipleship, required of every Christian, and ministry as the activity of someone authorized to represent the Church as it continues the ministry of Jesus Christ. The question we have to ask is: *Whose* ministry is this? Is it *my* ministry as a baptized Christian, or is it the Church's ministry? If everything I do out of my baptism is ministry, then Livingston is right, either the very category of ministry becomes problematic, or everything is ministry, or nothing is ministry. However, because the term *ministry* has become so common, we have collapsed the concept of discipleship into the concept of ministry.

Similarities and Differences

Deep similarities alongside differences in emphasis exist in the essays of James Bacik, Michael Downey, and Edward Hahnenberg. Bacik and Hahnenberg ground spirituality for Church ministers in baptism. Hahnenberg structures his essay through references to the rite of Christian initiation for adults, noting that baptism is a process implying growth and conversion. Bacik and Downey develop the Trinitarian dimensions of a baptismal ministerial spirituality.

Hahnenberg, in contrast to Livingston, is very clear in identifying ministry as a form of leadership that is ecclesial and public. Thus ministerial spirituality is also ecclesial, challenging "the minister to work *with* the Church and not simply *for* it." This requires accepting the Church's mission as one's own and representing the larger Church beyond the parish. This acceptance is not necessarily uncritical, but requires the asceticism of trying to understand Church decisions, presenting them fairly, and opening oneself to being formed by both the voices of leadership and the voices of the people in the pews. Hahnenberg's view of spirituality is neither individualistic nor private, but relational, ecclesial, and priestly. The priesthood of the baptized originating in baptism is a life lived in total response to God, a lifelong gift of self. Finally, as a *mystagogue*, that is, as someone who explains the rites of initiation after we have experienced them, the minister does not bring God to people, but names the grace in our lives, helps us to discover and understand what we have already received.

As I read Hahnenberg's essay, I think of John the Baptist saying, "He must increase, but I must decrease" (John 3:30). The minister must put aside ego in the discipline of thinking with the Church, must not cling to her own experience of grace in order to name and point out the grace of another. This movement from self to Church and the other, rather than conversion from sin to grace, is the "turn" implied in the ministerial conversion and transformation modeled on Christian initiation. Spiritual formation for the minister is "not only education, but real conversion and transformation" that takes place in community through the example and help of others.

James Bacik identifies all official ministry as a specification of the baptismal vocation shared with all Christians. Noting that spirituality "is hard to define in the abstract," he prefers to discuss it functionally. Because it is baptismal, it is Trinitarian in common with all baptized Christians. Trinitarian spirituality (1) depends on God in serving the kingdom, although never understanding or fully knowing God, (2) puts on the mind of Christ and enters into the paschal mystery of his death and resurrection, and (3) receives the gifts of the Spirit for the common good. Bacik defines the spiritual quest in Trinitarian terms: "union with the Father, through the incarnate Son in the power of the Holy Spirit." All Christian spirituality is incarnational since we "meet God in the concrete particularities of everyday life."

Only after a minister shares this spirituality with all the baptized can the particularity of ministerial spirituality be identified. Bacik, like Hahnenberg, locates the distinctive character of ministerial spirituality in the special position of ministers within the Church so that it "displays a thick ecclesial texture." He outlines the functional responsibilities of such ecclesial responsibility, but, unlike Hahnenberg, does not develop the spiritual implications of that. Instead, Bacik warns against the dangers of cynicism and "ecclesiolotry," the latter defined as "the tendency to make an idol out of the Church," and the failure to distinguish between the Church and the reign of God. He reminds Church ministers of the valuable resources the Catholic tradition has to contribute to postmodern culture: "a communal sense of human existence that challenges rugged individualism; a tradition of asceticism that counters consumerism; a natural-law ethic that opposes total relativism;

and a rich spiritual tradition that exposes the superficiality of our materialistic culture."

One of the differences shaping the different approaches ~~balk~~ to ministerial spirituality is whether we develop a spirituality ~~end~~ that we bring to ministry or whether the very fact of engaging authentically in ministry shapes our spirituality. Bacik assumes the latter position, noting that ministerial spirituality is both situational and structured. Ministerial activities can be catalysts for spiritual growth. Yet ministers must also structure their spiritual growth with the help of traditional spiritual practices, such as participation in the sacraments, prayer, Scripture study, and retreats.

Rooted in Baptism and Praise

Michael Downey describes a Trinitarian spirituality rooted in baptism. He defines spirituality broadly as likeness to Christ and communion with God and others rather than identifying it with prayer, discernment, or ascetic practice. Problems associated with ministerial spirituality occur when a minister—lay or ordained—tries to define his or her ministerial identity in contrast to the others and focuses on ministerial skills. A broadly based baptismal spirituality is common to all ministries, writes Downey, as they participate in the mission of Word and Spirit in making God's love evident and in participating in its unitive power.

Downey defines ministry relationally, commenting that all ministers are equal, although they differ in terms of their particular relationship to the Church and have their own activities and areas of responsibility. This leaves unexplained the meaning of *Lumen gentium's* description of the Church as being hierarchically structured (*L.G.*, chap. 3). The word *hierarchical* does not mean "higher," but means to have one's source in the holy or sacred. Nevertheless, more explanation is needed to show how the essential difference between ordained and lay ministry can be explained relationally, priests and bishops acting in a relationship of headship and other ministers relating as other members of the body of Christ. All are hierarchical in the sense of having their source in the sacred. The difference is indeed relational, but the head is not the hand, which is not the elbow, and so on. To be relational is not to be interchangeable. Downey is correct in rooting both ordained ministry and lay ministry in baptism, however. As one bishop at Vatican II observed, the sacramental character imparted in ordination does not erase the sacramental character imparted in baptism.

Downey's most profound insight is his observation that the Trinitarian and baptismal spirituality of ministry must, in the last analysis, be doxological. This means that the very form of our living and being and serving must be worship of God. We miss the essence of ministry if we think it is being set apart for service or identified by specific ministerial tasks. Ministry is praise of God and service to the Church. Fed by meditation on the word of God in Scripture and strengthened in sacrament, the baptized engage in witness, worship, and service as ways of being and building up the body of Christ.

If Downey's last statement is true of all the baptized, however, and if they, too, are members of the body of Christ and have a specific relationship within the body, Downey does not distinguish between ordained ministry, lay ecclesial ministry, and Christian discipleship. Even though all ministers, being baptized, share in a baptismal spirituality, the question remains whether ministerial spirituality has any characteristics in addition to this. This is where Hahnenberg offers a helpful ecclesial public dimension to a definition of ministry.

A Life of Prayer for the World

Ronald Rolheiser takes yet another step, moving from spirituality described in terms of the self and the Church to the world, the world being larger than the minister or the Church. Ministers are called to turn from their self-concerns and be "food for the life of the world," to build community, and to stand in solidarity with the poor. Rolheiser says that "the biggest danger in ministry is not so much that we will burn out, but that we will be too self-concerned and too self-protective to live the vulnerability that lies at the heart of Jesus' ministry." This spirituality requires the asceticism of being willing to bracket one's own temperaments, ideologies, and ecclesiologies in order to be compassionate like Jesus even when this leads us beyond orthodoxy, program, tradition, cause, and doctrine.

Rolheiser advocates asking the scary question: "What would Jesus do?" This, of course, always requires a delicate balance and prudent judgment. Doctrine does matter as does sound pastoral practice. Perhaps this is not so much putting doctrine aside as discerning a "hierarchy of truths" within doctrine, some doctrines being more foundational than other doctrines. Nevertheless, Rolheiser urges us not to be legalistic or stingy with God's grace.

So how does one do all this—feed the world, build community, stand with the poor, and put aside one's own agenda? The answer lies in affective prayer. Only when we can hear God saying unconditionally "I love you," can we be freed from our own efforts to make ourselves lovable, worthwhile, and immortal.

Perspectives on Ministerial Spirituality

Each one of the perspectives in this volume leaves us with a profound and unique truth in spite of similarities and differences. Donnelly shows us the value of discernment and the importance of listening to the gravitational pull that reveals God's particular will for us. Livingston discovers that ministers do not have the corner on spirituality, but share the pattern of the paschal mystery of dying and rising with all Christians. Bacik points to the incarnational essence of spirituality. Our spirituality is shaped in the very "doing" of ministry. Hahnenberg finds the distinctiveness of ministerial spirituality in its ecclesial character of representing the Church to others. Downey finds that it is doxological praise of the Triune God. Rolheiser locates it as grounded in the affective experience of God's love for us so that we can set our needs aside and be for the world and for the poor.

Putting them all together, what do we learn?

First, a minister does not cease being a Christian among Christians. Although a minister may have additional responsibilities, the pattern of Christ's death and rising assumed in the waters of baptism, the call to be in relationship and to praise God are shared with everyone trying to live a Christian life. First and foremost, a minister is baptized and lives out of that baptism.

Second, there is a distinction between Christian discipleship and ministry in a formal sense. A minister is authorized to represent the Church in a public way and therefore becomes a "public" person. A minister must fairly present the Church to those receiving ministry, putting aside personal agendas and ideologies. Ultimately, it is not "my" ministry, but the Church's ministry.

Third, the Church has a mission to the world. Spirituality can never be just between a minister and God or just about the Church. It must be missionary in scope, not in the narrow sense of soliciting members of the Church, but in the broad sense of working that the reign of God may be established. Paradoxically, even as the minister is sent out in the broadest possible way, sustenance is found in the most intimate experience of God's love. The most active missionary must be the most profound contemplative.

Ministry is about relationships and ministerial spirituality is relational in imitation of the Trinitarian relationships. The relationships are multiple: with God, with self, with the Church, with the world. Ministry serves communion.

Finally, ministerial spirituality is about "putting on Christ," discerning the gifts of the Holy Spirit, and worshiping the Father with our very lives. Ministerial spirituality is lifelong formation and conversion. We become ministers over a lifetime as we become Christians over a lifetime. We will never cease beginning again in the spiritual life and looking for help on that journey.